T0130169

53

Interesting **Things** to do in your Seminars and **Tutorials**

Tips and strategies for running really effective small groups

Hannah Strawson, Sue Habeshaw,
Trevor Habeshaw and Graham Gibbs

Routledge
Taylor & Francis Group

LONDON AND NEW YORK

First published in Australia and New Zealand by Allen & Unwin in 2012
This edition published in the United Kingdom in 2012 by The Professional and
Higher Partnership

Based on an earlier edition by Sue Habeshaw, Graham Gibbs and Trevor
Habeshaw, first published in 1984 by Technical and Educational Services Ltd.
Revised and updated for this edition by Hannah Strawson.

First published 2012 by Allen & Unwin

Published 2020 by Routledge
2 Park Square, Milton Park, Abingdon, Oxon OX14 4RN
605 Third Avenue, New York, NY 10017

Routledge is an imprint of the Taylor & Francis Group, an informa business

Cataloguing-in-Publication details are available
from the National Library of Australia
www.trove.nla.gov.au

ISBN-13: 9781743311585 (pbk)

Contents

Titles in the series   vi
Foreword   vii
Preface to the first edition   xi

Chapter 1   Starting off   1
1   Getting to know you   3
2   Learning names   5
3   A group agreement   7
4   Ground rules   9
5   Objectives   11
6   Orientation   13
7   Starting again   15

Chapter 2   Student-led seminars   17
8   Preparing groups for seminars   19
9   Briefing seminar leaders   21
10 Supporting seminar leaders   23
11 Feedback to seminar leaders   25
12 Self and peer evaluation   27

Chapter 3   Groupwork   29
13 Breaking up the group   31
14 Breaking up the task   33
15 Sub-groups   35
16 Line-up   37
17 Pyramid   39
18 Debate   41
19 Furniture   43
20 Rearranging the furniture   45

Chapter 4   Encouraging students to participate   47
21   Getting students to speak   49
22   Rounds   53
23   Gifts   55
24   Students' questions   57
25   Students' interests   59
26   Thought shower   61
27   Buzzer   63
28   Open and closed questions   65
29   Getting students to stop speaking   67

Chapter 5   Encouraging students to take responsibility   69
30   Distribute group roles   71
31   Working alone   73
32   Leave the room   75
33   Carry on without me   77
34   Self-help groups   79
35   A new teacher   81
36   Group grades   83

Chapter 6   Evaluating the work of the group   85
37   Group self-monitoring   87
38   Observers   89
39   Checking it out   91
40   Record your tutorial   93
41   Consulting the group   95

Chapter 7   Written material   97
42   Display   99
43   Group charts   101
44   Students' notes   103
45   Handouts   105
46   Writing   107
47   Open-book tutorials   109
48   Essay preparation   111
49   Coursework feedback   113

Chapter 8   Expressing feelings   **115**
50   What's on top   117
51   Self disclosure   119
52   Praise and encouragement   121
53   Concluding   123

Titles in the series

53 Interesting Things to do in your Lectures
53 Interesting Things to do in your Seminars and Tutorials
53 Interesting Ways of Helping your Students to Study

Foreword

The original edition of *53 interesting things to do in your seminars and tutorials* was published in a series called 'Interesting ways to teach'. It was written by Sue Habeshaw, Graham Gibbs and Trevor Habeshaw – all of them experienced teachers – and published by their company, Technical and Educational Services. The book proved popular amongst peers in post-compulsory education and ran to several editions.

Now that the original authors have retired from teaching, we are very pleased to have acquired from them the rights to this and other titles from that series. Much of the original material remains fresh and helpful. The text has, however, been revised and updated where appropriate. This task has been performed by Hannah Strawson. In two places (items 35 and 49), the original text has been replaced wholesale.

Anthony Haynes & Karen Haynes
The Professional and Higher Partnership Ltd

Preface to the first edition

This is the second of a series of books, each of which suggests practical ways of going about various aspects of teaching. All the ideas we offer have worked for us or for our colleagues: they are all tried and tested ways of doing things. You are probably familiar with some of them already. While there are sound theoretical justifications for these methods (and occasionally even empirical evidence in their support), they are offered here simply as ideas worth trying for yourself. We find them rewarding to use. We hope that you find some of them equally rewarding.

This book is not meant to be read from start to finish, but rather to be dipped into. Although the suggestions are grouped under headings, and are cross-referenced, they are written so that each makes sense on its own. Each one follows a similar pattern: a statement of the problem or issue it addresses, a description of the method, and, where this seems helpful, examples of its use and suggestions for dealing with possible difficulties. Where appropriate we have made reference to original sources of ideas or to places where fuller explanations can be found.

Many of the suggestions in this book are based on principles which may be new to your students. If they are not accustomed to taking responsibility for their own learning, for example, or expressing their feelings in the group, they will need time to get used to the idea. When introducing them to a new method, you can help them by telling them what is involved, explaining why you think it's worth doing and giving them time to think about it and talk it through in the group.

Graham Gibbs, Sue Habeshaw, Trevor Habeshaw

Chapter 1

Starting off

1 Getting to know you   3

2 Learning names   5

3 A group agreement   7

4 Ground rules   9

5 Objectives   11

6 Orientation   13

7 Starting again   15

1

1 Getting to know you

The sooner members of your tutorial group get to know each other, the sooner they will feel easy about working together and participating in discussion. If you spend some time on introductory exercises at the beginning of a course, students will feel that they have made a start in getting to know each other.

There are three sorts of exercise you can do: individual, in pairs, or in small groups. (Whichever you do, don't forget to join in yourself.)

a   **Individual**
    Each person introduces herself and says something about herself. It's helpful if you make explicit what this should be and write it on the board.

    It could be:
    – my name
    – where I'm from, and
    – why I'm here

    or,
    – my name
    – which options I'm doing, and
    – who else I know in this room.

b   **Pairs**
    Group members get into pairs and spend three minutes each finding out about their partner. At the end of the six minutes, each person introduces her partner to the rest of the group and tells them something about her.

c   **Small groups**
    Students form groups of three or four and spend five minutes
    finding out what they've got in common with the others in
    their group: taste in music, 'A' levels, Auntie Annies, and so
    on. At the end of five minutes they report to the other groups
    what they have in common.

One advantage of this type of exercise is that it ensures that everybody has the experience of speaking early on. If you want your
students to get used to speaking in tutorials, the sooner they start
the better.

If individuals join your tutorial group late, don't forget to organise introductions for them. You could say, for example, 'This is
Chris, who's transferred from another course. I'd like to welcome
you to this group. Who do you know here? . . . Perhaps the rest of
you would like to tell Chris who you are and say something about
yourselves. (I'll draw a plan of the room with the names on, Chris,
to help you remember who everyone is.) And then we'll ask you to
say something about yourself. OK, who'd like to start?'

2 Learning names

Members of a group cannot work together successfully if they don't know each others' names. When you meet a new group, find out if they know each other, and if they don't, spend some time working on names.

If you have started with some kind of introductory exercise, they will already have heard each others' names. You can build on this in the following ways:

a   Get students in turn to say the names of everyone in the group and join in yourself. Then change places and do it again until all the names are familiar.

b   On the board draw a plan of the furniture in the room and as students speak, write in each name at the appropriate point on the plan.

c   Ask students to say their own name first when they speak in the group for the first few times and when they form pairs ask them to remind their partner of their name.

d   Encourage them to ask when they forget someone's name.

e   Use students' names yourself when you speak to them.

Students find these activities potentially embarrassing but often remark later how quickly the group gelled as a result.

3 A group agreement

In educational institutions the expectations of students are usually meticulously specified while the teachers have more flexibility and choice. For example, in most institutions deadlines are set for the submission of students' course work but not for its return by the teachers.

If you want to make the situation more equitable you can negotiate a group agreement with your students. The first time you meet your tutorial groups you can say, 'There are all kinds of regulations governing your behaviour on this course and these are all spelt out in the course handbook. (For instance . . .) There aren't any regulations for me. I'd like us to spend some time today drawing up some rules which will specify what you expect of me and what I expect of you. Shall we start with a round of suggestions?' (see item **22**). These suggestions then form the basis for negotiating the group agreement.

The agreement could be, for example, 'You will submit your course work by the cut-off date and I will return it to you, marked, within x days of your cut-off date' or 'You will do the preparatory reading for each tutorial and I will provide guidelines for each set of reading' or 'We all agree to be here at x o'clock each week, ready to start'.

Normally, the very existence of a group agreement, if it has been freely entered into by all parties, ensures that it will be honoured. If it is broken, however, group members need to feel free to remind each other of the agreement and feel willing to accept reminders from others. You can aid this by encouragement and by example.

4 Ground rules

All groups have ground rules though usually these are not made specific. Tutorial groups normally have unspoken ground rules relating to the role of the teacher (as, for example, 'It is the job of the teacher to devise the tutorial programme, open and close the tutorials, etc.') and ground rules relating to the behaviour of the students (as, for example, 'Students are not allowed to interrupt the teacher though they are allowed to interrupt other students'). These ground rules are based on authoritarian teaching methods and actively discourage student participation.

If, instead of leaving your ground rules unspoken, you give some time at the beginning of the course to specifying them, you have the opportunity to ensure that the group has the ground rules it wants rather than a set of rules based on false assumptions and traditions.

Students who are unused to setting their own ground rules may find it difficult at first to see what you mean and will be wary of making suggestions. They may find it helpful if you take the activity in two stages: first explain the principle of ground rules and together make a preliminary list; then, after one or more tutorials, ask them, in the light of their experience, what changes they would like to make to the list.

Their list could look something like this:

Ground rules for this group:

a   Don't interrupt other people
b   It's OK to opt out and opt in again
c   Anyone can suggest changing or adding to the ground rules at any time

d   Every group member is entitled to time
e   It's OK to ask other people for help
f   At any point anyone can suggest that the group moves on
g   We start on the hour and finish at ten minutes to

The best way of ensuring that the ground rules are kept is for group members to be scrupulous from the outset about reminding people when they break them. It is important that you as a teacher don't see yourself as being above the law: you should encourage students to remind you if you break a ground rule and accept the reminder when they do.

See also **3 A group agreement**.

Some of the activities referred to in other parts of this book have their own ground rules. These are specified where they occur.

5 Objectives

Teachers frequently specify their educational objectives for course submissions, prospectuses, etc. These objectives are usually well written and, because they focus on behaviour and skills, give a clearer idea of what is expected of students than can be gained from syllabuses, tutorial programmes or reading lists. So it seems a pity that they are so rarely shown to the students.

If you have already worked out objectives for your courses, it will be a very quick job to make copies of them for your tutorial groups. The times when students will probably be most receptive to them will be at the beginning of the course, when they are trying to orientate themselves, and at the end, when they are focusing on the examinations.

6 Orientation

You and your students come to the tutorial from various other activities and events and from various parts of the building or even from outside. It is probably a week since this group of people met in this place for this purpose. So you need an orientation period. If you start the tutorial before you are all oriented, you will not have your students' full attention and they will not have yours.

The simplest methods of orientation are based on increasing everyone's awareness of the room, the people and the purpose of the tutorial. So it is helpful to spend some time arranging the furniture in the room to suit the group (see item **19**), putting up posters, writing the programme on the board and so on.

If you get to the room first, you can greet the students by name as they arrive. You can spend time chatting about the course with students as you wait for late-comers. And then, at the start of the tutorial, you can orientate students to this week's work by relating it to last week's and to the total programme and quickly running through what you hope will be achieved today. And in time you can encourage students to orientate themselves, maybe by reviewing last week's tutorial with a neighbour, or by taking some responsibility for the arrangement of the furniture or the drawing up of the programme.

7 Starting again

Students return to courses in two ways: to start the second or third year, or to resume college work after a period of placement.

It can be helpful formally to acknowledge this 'restart' in some way in order to:

a   bring the group together again as a cohesive unit,

b   enable any unfinished business from the past to be cleared up, and

c   signify moving forward to a further stage.

Two examples will illustrate this process:

Rounds (see item 22)

a   One thing I liked about last year was …
     and one thing I didn't like was …

b   The best thing about my placement was …
     and the worst thing was …

c   I think my performance on the course last year was …
     This year I would like to …

Pyramid (see item 17)

a   **Individually**
     Students write one list headed 'Good things about my placement', and a similar list of 'Bad things about my placement' (10 minutes).

b **Pairs**
   Students show their lists to their neighbours (5 minutes).

c **Fours**
   Each person has five minutes to describe her placement, explain what work she did and answer questions from other members of the group (20 minutes).

d **Plenary round**
   'The main thing I got from my placement was . . .' (This will take one to two minutes per person.)

An additional benefit of this exercise is that it offers some informal feedback to the teacher about the placements.

Chapter 2

Student-led seminars

8 Preparing groups for seminars   19

9 Briefing seminar leaders   21

10 Supporting seminar leaders   23

11 Feedback to seminar leaders   25

12 Self and peer evaluation   27

8 Preparing groups for seminars

When you are embarking on a series of seminars in which students will present papers and lead discussions, you can be very helpful to the group if you spend some time talking about problems of student seminars, organising the programme and identifying what part everyone is to play.

If this is a new venture for the students or if they have had bad experiences in the past, it's a good idea to give them a chance to talk about their worries. A round of 'The worst thing that could happen when it's my turn to lead the seminar' (see item 22), followed by the pooling of suggested ways of avoiding these crises, will be reassuring for them.

When organising the programme, you can be helpful to students if you give them the widest possible choice of date and topic. Indeed, this is something you may be able to leave entirely to them. If you give them a list of dates and topics and leave the room (see item 32), this will help to accustom them in a small way to making decisions for themselves instead of always deferring to you. Alternatively, you could assign topics to different students and tell them the week in which you want them to be a group leader, or you could simply pick the topics and dates out of a hat. Whichever method you choose, it is generally a good idea to allow the students to switch topics and dates between themselves.

You will need to make it clear to the group that, in a student-led seminar, the immediate responsibility for the session rests with the student leader and that your role will alter correspondingly. If the session is to be a success the members of the group must accept these new roles. This is a difficult adjustment for them to make and they will need help. You could say, 'Next week Rosie will be leading the seminar and I shall be a member of the group like anyone else. People will probably find it helpful, Rosie, if you sit here next week, in front of the board where I usually sit. It'll be up to you, Rosie, to decide how the seminar is organised and when to start and finish. How do you feel about that?' Of course this will only work if during Rosie's seminar you resist all temptations or invitations to take over.

9 Briefing seminar leaders

Students who are to lead a seminar are usually expected to do the preparation for it on their own. If, however, you offer individual students the facility of discussing their seminar with you beforehand, this will give them an opportunity to try out some of their ideas and give you the chance to offer practical suggestions and support.

When they come to see you, they will probably have a fairly clear idea about the content of the seminar but will not have thought about the process. You can be helpful by suggesting that they:

a   list their objectives (see item 5);

b   consider what methods they are going to use to involve the other group members (see, for example, items 22 and 24);

c   draw up an outline plan for the session to include the methods they are going to use (see, for example, items 13 and 14), and an estimate of the timing;

d   list the questions which they intend to put to the group (see item 28). They will find it helpful if they make a list of direct questions, in inverted commas, rather than a list of question topics;

e   make copies of their presentation/handout material as appropriate.

Time spent at this stage is never wasted.

10 Supporting seminar leaders

A student who is leading a seminar will need your help in adopting and carrying through her new role.

You can help her in specific ways, for example, by sitting in a different seat and letting her sit in the place near the board and, in particular, by not talking too much yourself. Indeed, you may like to try keeping totally silent for the first half hour, say, or even try staying away from the first seminar altogether to give the group a chance to adapt to student leadership.

If the seminar leader does appeal to you to take over some of the responsibility by asking you when she should start or what she should do next, you can pass the responsibility back gently by saying, 'This is your seminar, Rosie. It's up to you'.

If she gets into serious difficulties and dries up or gets totally confused, there are two kinds of help you can give her. The short-term solution, which is humiliating for the student and likely to undermine her confidence for future such occasions, is to take over the seminar yourself. Long-term solutions, which enable her to continue for herself, are to prompt her by saying, 'You were talking about x' or, if she has panicked, to say firmly, 'It's OK, Rosie. Carry on'. You can talk about this further when you are giving her feedback later (see item 11).

11 Feedback to seminar leaders

Leading a seminar can be a frightening and potentially upsetting experience for students and one in which they often find it difficult to evaluate their own performance. If you set up the opportunity for the seminar leader to evaluate herself and get feedback from the group or from you, the seminar is more likely to be a positive learning experience for her.

If the members of the group feel comfortable with each other, they may give feedback to the seminar leader quite spontaneously without being asked. If they don't, or if their comments are a bit vague ('Very good' or 'Well done!'), you will need to set up a structure for them.

One simple structure is the round (see item 22) in which all the group members, including the seminar leader and you, say one thing they liked about the seminar. This guarantees positive feedback from everybody in the group and ensures that the comments are fuller and more specific than just 'very good'. It also gives everyone some extra practice in evaluating.

Another similar structure is self and peer evaluation (see next item).

If you have the facilities, you could video record the student's performance for her to watch back in her own time. This will allow her to privately critically evaluate the work she has done. However, be sure to also provide her with feedback in another form in case she does not like watching herself on screen, or in case there are areas of improvement that she is unable to spot herself.

If you decide to give feedback to the seminar leader in a one-to-one session afterwards, be sure to invite her to evaluate herself first: this is not only better for her self-respect but also encourages her to develop skills of self-evaluation, an important prerequisite for improvement. When you give your feedback, don't underestimate how powerful a person you are in her life and be sure to balance negative feedback with at least as much that is positive.

12 Self and peer evaluation

This method can be used in a seminar or in any situation where the group is to give feedback to one of its members.

It consists of a round (see item 22) in which everyone, including the seminar leader and the member of staff, says one positive thing and one negative thing about the seminar. It is helpful if group members flag what they are saying by beginning, 'My positive feedback to you is ...' and 'My negative feedback to you is ...'.

There are strict rules for this activity as the situation is a delicate one.

a   Ground rules for the group members (see item 4)
1   Say one positive and one negative thing.
2   Do not interrupt anyone else or comment on anyone else's contribution.

b   Ground rules for the person whose performance is being evaluated
1   Evaluate yourself first: say something positive and something negative.
2   Listen to what is said without replying. (The reason for this is that if you reply you may concentrate on justifying yourself instead of listening to the feedback and selecting from it what is useful to you.)

It is also helpful if one group member writes down what is said. This is so that the subject can listen carefully to each speaker and still have a copy of the comments to look over at her leisure.

Chapter 3

Groupwork

13 Breaking up the group   31

14 Breaking up the task   33

15 Sub-groups   35

16 Line-up   37

17 Pyramid   39

18 Debate   41

19 Furniture   43

20 Rearranging the furniture   45

13 Breaking up the group

However small a group is, there are occasions when it is too big to tackle a particular task effectively. Even a group of two can be too big when faced with a new and complex problem, or a pile of unfamiliar literature. Once a tutorial group has been set up, however, there is a tendency to keep working in that size group whatever is being done.

It can be much more effective to alter the group size according to the task in hand. A group of eight might work best as an eight for pooling ideas and making democratic decisions, in two fours for generating ideas and reacting to proposals, in four twos for detailed work and the trying out of half-formed ideas, and as eight individuals for 'leg work', reading, calculations, etc.

Try to recognise when a group seems to be too big for the task in hand and be bold in proposing smaller working units. This can be invaluable for even very short periods.

You could say, for example, 'We seem to be struggling with this plan a bit. Maybe it is too much to take on all at once. There are four main sections to the plan. I suggest that you form four groups of three and take one section each. Section one group here . . . section two group here . . . OK? I'll give you five minutes in your groups and see how you progress. Then I'll either give you longer or bring us back together. Remember the question is "What would be the likely consequences if this plan were to be introduced?"'

See also the following items:

14 Breaking up the task
15 Sub-groups
17 Pyramid
20 Rearranging the furniture.

14 Breaking up the task

Some topics are so big or abstract or complex that groups have difficulty handling them unless the discussion is structured in some way. A simple way of structuring the discussion is to divide the topic into component parts and distribute them among members of the group. For example, students on a social work or community psychiatric nursing course could examine the topic of ageing from the various angles of biology, psychology, sociology, social policy and health education. Or students of history could research separately into different commentators on the industrial revolution.

The component parts can be presented in the form of a list of topic sub-headings, questions, problems, quotations, etc. Students choose one item and work on it singly or in pairs for an agreed length of time. The group then comes together and hears the report on each item. Finally the group has an open discussion on the topic as a whole.

It is important that sufficient time is allowed for piecing the topic together again. **Jig-saw**, an alternative name for the method, recognises this.

The advantages of this method over open discussion are not only that the topic is covered more fully but also that all students are bound to participate and the standard of their contributions is likely to be higher because they have had time to think.

Incidentally, this method can serve as a model for structuring material in the writing of essays, notes, etc.

See also **13 Breaking up the group**.

15 Sub-groups

The activities covered in **Chapter 3** (items **13** to **20**) involve dividing your tutorial group into sub-groups. This item describes two specific kinds of sub-group – **buzz** and **syndicate groups** – and summarises their different uses.

a   **Buzz groups**

Buzz groups are pairs or small groups of students who are assigned a task or discussion topic for a limited period (often 5 minutes or less) within the tutorial. The name comes from the noise which is generated when students start talking in buzz groups.

A good moment to suggest buzz is when you want all members of your tutorial group to reflect actively on something, particularly in the area of their personal response or experience. You could say, 'Talk with your neighbour for a couple of minutes about where you stand on this issue' or 'Can you think of applications of this principle to your own experience? Get into groups of three and discuss it' or 'What do you think of it so far? Tell your neighbour'.

This discussion can be sufficient in itself and need not entail any reporting back afterwards.

b   **Syndicate groups**

Syndicate groups, or problem centered group, are small groups of students (4 to 6 is ideal) who are assigned a problem to work on in the tutorial. In the case of a complex problem, an entire session, or several sessions, can be devoted to syndicate group work. Students can be encouraged to use the library, the internet and other resources to help them with the problem. The teacher, too, can be available as a resource. On completing the problem, groups report back to the teacher and to the other students.

Working in syndicate groups gives your students the opportunity to try out new ideas and methods in a sub-group where they are confronted with alternative suggestions and receive immediate feedback. Reporting back enables them to compare a range of possible solutions to the problem.

16 Line-up

When doing group work (see items **13**, **14** and **15**), you will probably find from time to time that you need to reorganise the sub-groups so that students mix and work with a range of other people. Line-up is a way of doing this which is more positive than just saying vaguely, 'Er, can you get into new groups?' It's also more fun.

In a line-up, students line themselves up across the room according to an agreed criterion and then divide into sub-groups according to their position in the line. You can choose a criterion which is unrelated to the work of the tutorial (hair colour, height, place of birth, etc.) or one which is related to the work of the tutorial (amount of relevant experience, etc.)

You could say, 'Before we move on to the next exercise, shall we mix the sub-groups? . . . OK, how about a line-up? . . . Can you all stand up, please? Let's make a line across the room, facing the window, from the person with the most experience of this topic at that end to the person with the least experience at this end. If you're not sure how your experience compares with other people's, then you'll have to talk to them and find out'.

When students have decided where to place themselves in the line, you can choose how they should divide into sub-groups. They can join up with their immediate neighbours, in which case you get groups of similar people together, or you can organise mixed groups: if you have twelve students, for example, and you want to form mixed groups of three, you ask the students to number off in fours – 1, 2, 3, 4; 1, 2, 3, 4; 1, 2, 3, 4 – and then all the 1's form a group, all the 2's form a group, etc.

Other benefits of this method are that it raises the energy of the group and that, depending on the criteria for line-up that you choose, it offers students a chance to evaluate themselves without feeling threatened.

17 Pyramid

The 'pyramid' or 'snowball' method involves students first working alone, then in pairs, then in fours and so on. Normally after working in fours they join in some form of whole group activity involving the pooling of their conclusions or solutions. The method was developed by Andrew Northedge[1] for use with tutorial groups.

The following example illustrates the type of activity which lends itself to pyramids. A guide to timing is given in brackets.

Stage 1 Individuals (5 minutes)
Students note down some questions of their own which relate to the tutorial topic.
You can judge for yourself which of your tutorial topics are suitable for pyramids but some examples might be:
(in economics) the fall of the pound against the dollar;
(in psychology) alternative therapies;
(in drama) the motivation of Hedda Gabler.

Stage 2 Pairs (10 minutes)
Pairs of students try to answer one another's questions.

Stage 3 Fours (20 minutes)
Pairs join together to make fours and, in the light of their discussion of the questions, identify general problems and areas of controversy in the tutorial topic.

Stage 4 Plenary (3 minutes for each representative)
A representative from each group of four reports the conclusions of her four to the group as a whole. These conclusions can be listed on the board as a record.

The cumulative structure of the pyramid carries with it a number of benefits:

- the early individual and paired work gives students the opportunity to try out their ideas on their own and with one other person before risking them with a larger number of people

- the progressive increase in group size means that students are repeatedly confronted with ideas and assumptions which are different from their own

- the graded increase in the complexity of the tasks, where each stage is built on the achievement of the previous stage, makes problems easier to handle.

With this in mind, you need to design your pyramid in such a way that students are doing something different at each stage: if you repeat the same task, they will get bored and feel that they aren't moving forward.

Pyramids for specific purposes are illustrated in:

7 **Starting again**
37 **Group self-monitoring**

See also 15 **Sub-groups**.

Reference
1 Northedge, A., 'Learning through Discussion in the Open University', in *Teaching at a Distance*, 2, 1975.

18 Debate

An important use of the tutorial is as an arena for debate. Teachers often get students to prepare for tutorials by reading statements of a variety of viewpoints in a controversial area. The problem in the tutorial frequently seems to be that in debating the topic students tend to leave the discussion to a small number of articulate, confident or aggressive students.

A way of involving all the students is to divide them into as many sub-groups as there are points of view in the controversial area and then to get each sub-group to prepare a case for its viewpoint. The debate itself can be organised quite informally. For example, you could say to a class of trainee teachers, 'Which of you think that behavioural objectives are a good idea? OK, would you people like to form a group on this side of the room and prepare a series of arguments for behavioural objectives? The rest of you are opposed to behavioural objectives, then, or aren't convinced? Can you get into a group, then, and prepare your arguments? In twenty minutes we'll come together and have the debate. What I shall do is ask each group in turn to make one statement which the other side will argue against. So you'll need to prepare your arguments in order of importance. Right, you've got twenty minutes'.

Some possible variations, which you can employ when students are accustomed to this kind of debate, are:

- students speak **for** a view which they don't agree with

- students **change sides** half way through the debate

- students **role play a proponent** of the view they support

These have the advantage of further improving students' skills in argument and increasing their capacity for understanding the other person's viewpoint.

19 Furniture

The arrangement of furniture in the classroom is probably the single most important factor in determining the success of the tutorial.

Unhelpful arrangements

a   If the teacher has a special desk, or a higher or larger chair, or even just a special place, this will give her added status and distance her from the students and will make it highly likely that she will dominate the session.

b   If students sit in rows facing the teacher, so that they cannot see one another's faces, this will prevent interaction between them and put all the responsibility for the session onto the teacher.

c   If there is too great a distance between the participants, or large obstructions between them, such as large tables, this will make it harder for them to communicate with each other and make it easy for individuals to avoid contributing.

d   If the teacher sits in front of the board which is used to display information, she then becomes the focus of attention and 'guardian of knowledge'.

e   If group members sit around a long table or in a long rectangle, especially if the teacher sits at one end, this tends to result in a focusing of attention on that end, while the students at the other end disengage or start their own discussion.

Helpful arrangements

a   Sit in a circle if at all possible, so that everyone can see and communicate with everyone else, with no seats having special status.

b   Think carefully about where you position yourself in relation to the board and leave a gap in front of it, so that any group member can feel free to use it.

c   Anticipate the possibility of breaking up into sub-groups for some of the time (see also items **13**, **15** and **20**).

d   Give sub-groups a physical identity by seating them together.

19 *Furniture*

20 Rearranging the furniture

Just as the arrangement of furniture needs to echo the activity of the group (see item **19**), so the furniture needs to be rearranged when the group activity changes.

For example, if students have been sitting in a circle or round a large table listening to an introductory briefing, they can find it difficult suddenly to engage in group work (see item **13**) with their immediate neighbours: the change of intellectual demands and change of social relations can be too great to accommodate. The transition will be eased if there is a corresponding alteration in the physical arrangement of the group. This can be achieved by students moving their chairs away from the table and into groups and then returning to the table for the pooling of ideas. If there is space, they can form their sub-groups in another part of the room or even in separate rooms.

Similarly, in a situation where students form two opposing groups, as in a debate (see item **18**), they can arrange themselves physically face to face in two groups, and then move back into a circle for the follow-up discussion.

Chapter 4

Encouraging students to participate

21 Getting students to speak   49

22 Rounds   53

23 Gifts   55

24 Students' questions   57

25 Students' interests   59

26 Thought shower   61

27 Buzzer   63

28 Open and closed questions   65

29 Getting students to stop speaking   67

21 Getting students to speak

Teachers often complain that they have difficulty getting students to speak in tutorials and students for their part may regard an invitation to participate as 'being picked on'. The main reason for this is that teachers and students alike seem to believe that while teachers can require students to read books, write essays and sit examinations, they don't have the right to ask them to speak. Other common reasons for students' reluctance to participate in a tutorial are that they don't know the ground rules (see item 4), they are afraid of exposing themselves in public, or simply that they sense that the teacher really wants to do all the talking.

If, however, you really want your students to speak and you believe you have the right to ask them to speak and you are looking for ways of making it easier for them, you could start by discussing expectations and ground rules. Exchange views about how you would like the tutorials to be, tell them about your plans for getting them to speak (see below), and specify any ground rules. For example, students often assume that there is a ground rule that all discussion should be conducted through the chair and that they should apologise if they speak directly to another student. If you want a free ranging discussion, you will need to introduce the opposite ground rule – 'Anyone is allowed to speak to anyone' – and demonstrate your support for it by the way you behave. You could emphasise its importance by giving the students some practice straight away. You could say, 'I'm aware that because I'm a member of staff, you tend to listen more to what I say and address your remarks to me rather than to others in the group. If you do this, the discussion never really gets off the ground and we waste the benefits of being in a group. So what I'd like to suggest is that I keep silent for the next half hour and you continue the discussion. You know enough about this topic to be able to do that quite easily. I shall sit here quietly but if I think my presence is inhibiting you, I'll leave the room for half an hour (see item 32). I'm going to stop speaking now'.

Students also tend to assume that the teacher is the only person who is allowed to invite people into the discussion, which is a pity because they often know more about their friends' special knowledge and interests than the teacher does. It's good to hear one student say to another, 'You know about this, don't you, Mandy? What was it you were saying yesterday?' You could encourage this by introducing a further ground rule: 'Anyone is allowed to bring another person into the discussion'.

Exercises which ensure that every student will speak fall into two categories. One is the type of exercise where students speak for themselves in turn:

Rounds (item 22)

Students' questions (item 24)

Self and peer evaluation (item 12)

The other is the type where a pair or small group of students talks together on a topic and then selects one member to act as rapporteur to the total group:

Sub-groups (item 15)

Pyramid (item 17)

Debate (item 18)

In both types of exercise students have time to think before exposing themselves to the whole group; in the second type they also have the opportunity to try out their ideas on one or two other students before presenting them to everybody.

You will find that when the students have spoken just once in one of these exercises, they will tend to be more willing to speak again in later unstructured discussions.

22 Rounds

One of the simplest ways of ensuring that all your students will speak in tutorials is to agree that rounds will form part of the regular activities of the group. In a round everyone in turn, including the teacher, makes a statement, uninterrupted, on a given topic. The topic can be proposed by any member of the group. It can relate to the subject matter of the tutorial or to group processes or to the feelings of the group members and can be planned in advance or devised in response to a situation as it arises.

Ground rules (see item 4) for rounds are:

- speak in turn, not out of turn

- it's OK to pass

- it's OK to repeat what someone else has already said.

Rounds are featured in a number of items in this book. Some examples are:

'My name, where I'm from, and why I'm here' (see item 1)

'What I would like to see included in this group agreement' (see item 3)

'I think my performance last year was . . . This year I'd like to . . .' (see item 7)

'The worst thing that could happen when it's my turn to lead the seminar' (see item 8)

'My positive feedback to you is . . . My negative feedback is . . .' (see item 12)

'What I'm taking away from this tutorial' (see item **44**)

'Something good my partner wrote in her essay' (see item **49**)

'What's on top' (see item **50**)

'One thing I like about being in this group' (see item **52**)

Advantages of the round are not only that it ensures that everyone speaks but also that it highlights the diversity of contributions and encourages students to learn from one another.

If you are worried that the round may take up too much of your tutorial time, you can, of course, set a time limit on each contribution.

23 Gifts

The more a student puts into a group, the more she gets out of it. A particular application of this principle is seen in the bringing of tangible gifts to the group. These gifts can vary depending on the course.

You could say to a group of law students, for example, 'Illustrations of what we've been talking about crop up in law reports in the newspapers and online all the time so what I suggest we do is all bring a relevant article to the next tutorial and I'll bring one too'.

Or, in an English literature tutorial, you could say, 'Next week we're going to start on the poetry of the First World War. Obviously I could bring along my choice of poems for us to work on but I'm sure you have all read war poems which have made an impression on you and I think it would be interesting and give more variety to the tutorial if you all brought a poem of your choice and said a few words about why you chose it. I'll bring one too'. (You can have spares available for students who don't bring gifts of their own but these are not generally needed.)

This kind of activity aids group cohesion and the establishment of a group identity. The students have actively participated in the shaping of the proceedings and feel good because they have given and received gifts.

24 Students' questions

Questions in tutorials are usually asked by teachers. There are several advantages in inviting your students to ask the questions for a change: one is that it gives them more responsibility; another is that the students are in the best position to identify those aspects of the tutorial material which puzzle or interest them; another is that they are gaining practice in a skill which they can then apply to asking questions as they are reading, listening to lectures or revising for exams.

Here are the descriptions of two simple procedures based on students' questions. Begin with everyone in the group, including the teacher, writing down a question based on the tutorial material. (It may be something they don't understand which they want explained or it may be a question to which they know the answer, in an area that interests them.) Then either (a) these are listed on the board and pairs of students select a question, their own or someone else's, to work on and at an agreed time report back to the rest of the group on their conclusions, or (b) individuals in turn ask their question and chair the discussion which lasts until they feel they have received a satisfactory answer.

25 Students' interests

Given the chance, students will express an interest in all sorts of things more or less related to the course. You can foster these interests in a number of ways: by showing enthusiasm yourself, by giving plenty of choice in the selection of seminar topics and essay titles, and by giving time for individual students' interests in the tutorials. You could say, for example, in response to a criticism that something isn't on the syllabus, 'No, that isn't on the syllabus and it's a pity in some ways. But if you're interested in it, Michael, would you like some time at the beginning of the next tutorial to talk to us about it and answer some of our questions?'

This needn't take a lot of time and is not a suggestion that you abandon your course to pursue an individual's interests but it does mean that you are showing respect for your students and may also suggest to you some ways in which you could extend and develop your course.

26 Thought shower

This is a very good method for the situation where the aim is to expand people's thinking in an area and look for ideas which might not be arrived at by rational methods. Because it is a situation where anything goes and people are not expected to justify what they say and also because they are stimulated by ideas coming from others, the results are often very creative. This method is particularly appropriate at the beginning of a course or section of a course: if the group surveys the area in the broadest possible way, they have a context into which to fit the detail and there is less likelihood that important items will be omitted.

In a thought shower members of the group call out suggestions which one member of the group – not necessarily the leader – writes down on a board, computer or flipchart.

The ground rules for the members are as follows:

- call out suggestions in any order

- don't explain or justify your suggestions

- don't comment on other people's suggestions

(These ground rules give group members the freedom to express their ideas, even if they aren't sure how they might explain or justify them.)

After an agreed period of time, or when no more suggestions are forthcoming, the group turns its attention to the total list, either accepting it as a statement of a range of possibilities (as in the first example below) or discussing the items and selecting the most useful (as in the second example below).

The procedure and ground rules will need to be made clear to the group before you start.

Two examples of the use of a thought shower:

a 'On this nineteenth-century novel course, we'll obviously be picking out different matters of interest from different novels but I think it's helpful if we agree before we start on the range of things we'll be looking out for in any novel that we read. So can we think about this? The title is *Things to look out for in a novel* and if you call them out, I'll write them up.'

b 'As trainee teachers it's crucial that you know how to evaluate your own teaching and what methods of evaluation you have to chose from. Can we make a thought shower on *Ways I can evaluate my teaching*? And then we'll pick out the ones we want to concentrate on.'

27 Buzzer

This is based on radio and television panel games where competitors press a buzzer to indicate that they want to speak.

It can be used in a situation where you want students to interrupt a recording or reading because it is full of points which they should be challenging and questioning. You could say, 'On this handout is an extract from . . . which deals with the topic we've just been discussing and I'm sure you'll find that you don't agree with everything the author says. So what I'm going to do is to start reading the passage aloud and I'd like you to press your buzzer when there is something you want to challenge'.

Students don't actually have a buzzer but they recognise the principle and readily interrupt, either with a verbal statement or, more usually, by saying '**Bzzz!**' (You could also get students to use a ring tone on their mobile phones – although you will run the risk of your students getting phone calls or messages during the seminar!) Once the interruption has been made, the group can then discuss the criticism more fully.

This activity has the effect of relaxing the group and encouraging participation, partly because it's fun and also because students can interrupt with a '**Bzzz!**' without needing to have formulated their precise criticism. And, perhaps most importantly, they feel free to interrupt precisely because this is an interruption exercise. Using this method also means that the group is following through the article or recording as a joint experience and dealing with the criticisms in context.

28 Open and closed questions

Since the most usual method used by a teacher to get students to speak is to ask them questions, it's helpful to know something about types of question and their likely effect.

There are several ways of categorising questions. A simple but useful one is the open/closed dimension which groups questions according to how much scope the student has in answering. A closed question gives the student very little scope: 'What is the formula for nitrous oxide?' or 'What was the date of the Battle of Borodino?' An open question allows more freedom: 'How would you suggest we put this hypothesis to the test?' or 'Can you say something about the Battle of Borodino?'

Both sorts of question are obviously useful and have their place in teaching but the mistake that many teachers make is to suppose that closed questions are easier to answer. It's true that they're usually quicker to answer and depend on lower order skills but in fact students find them more worrying and therefore are less likely to reply. The reason for this is that the answer is usually right or wrong which means that there is a higher risk of being seen to be wrong. So teachers who try to get the tutorial going with a few quick closed questions may effectively silence the students, particularly if they claim that their questions are easy, because then students have more to lose if they get an easy question wrong. A set of open questions, on the other hand, will draw students out.

If, during the orientation period at the start of the tutorial (see item 6), you use open questions in chatting to the students, they are then tuned in to answering open questions even before the tutorial has properly started. Such questions could be 'How did you get on with the reading?' or 'What did you think of the lecture?' or, simply, 'How's it going?'

29 Getting students to stop speaking

Highly articulate or garrulous students can be as much of a problem as quiet, reserved ones. The trouble is that such students tend either to intimidate or antagonise the other students and discourage them from joining in. The situation is often complicated by the fact that teachers will encourage such students early on because they are so relieved to have someone in the group who is willing to speak.

There are several possible ways of handling this situation:

a   Distribute the speaking time among the students by using one of the methods where everyone is expected to speak (see item 21).

b   When setting up sub-groups (see item 15), invite the students to identify themselves as 'higher contributors' or 'lower contributors' and then suggest that the higher contributors work together and the lower contributors work together.

c   Set up a situation at the beginning of each tutorial or for half an hour during a tutorial in which nobody speaks for a second time until everyone has spoken once. You will need first to explain to the group why you are doing this: that you have noticed that some people are speaking a lot and some people a little and that you want to try to redress the balance.

d   If you have such a serious problem with an individual that none of the above suggestions work, then you will have to confront her on her own, explain how you feel about her behaviour and ask her to change it, offering your help if she needs it.

Chapter 5

Encouraging students to take responsibility

30 Distribute group roles   71

31 Working alone   73

32 Leave the room   75

33 Carry on without me   77

34 Self-help groups   79

35 A new teacher   81

36 Group grades   85

30 Distribute group roles

One way of encouraging students to take more responsibility for the group without overburdening them is to identify the tasks involved in running a discussion group and assign them to individuals. This sharing of managerial roles can also lessen the social awkwardness involved when peers take charge of a group.

Typical roles could be:

> agenda fixer
> chairperson
> timekeeper
> monitor
> summariser
> note taker

Typical interventions for each role might be:

a   *Agenda fixer:* 'From what you have said there seem to be four main things to discuss: 1, 2, 3, 4. I suggest that we take them in order and start with 1, if that's OK.'

b   *Chairperson:* 'Thanks for that contribution, Dan. What do you think, Yasmin?'

c   *Timekeeper:* 'We've spent about 20 minutes on this point. Shall we move on?'

d   *Monitor:* 'I've noticed that contributions to the seminar have been uneven so far: some people have spoken a lot less than others. What do you suggest we do about it?'

e   *Summariser:* 'So it looks as though we're agreed that . . .'

f   *Note taker:* 'Hang on, Yasmin. Can I just get that written down, before we go on?'

31 Working alone

It is frequently assumed that a discussion session should consist of continuous talk and that working alone is for private study time. Yet giving students – and yourself – the chance to think alone, read alone, tackle a problem alone, etc. can be very valuable for short periods at various stages during a tutorial and even during a one-to-one tutorial.

Even one minute of such activity can dramatically improve the subsequent working of the group.

32 Leave the room

Many of the ideas described in this book give the teacher a relatively small role: chairperson, timekeeper, etc. And for at least some of the time the teacher is actually redundant. It can then be quite disruptive to those who are working (on their own or in small groups) if there is someone present who is obviously not working. If the teacher is walking around, observing, or sitting in on small groups, this can be distracting to those who are working. Even sitting quietly out of the way, getting on with other work, can be quite inhibiting to students. The smaller the total size of the group, the more inhibiting this is likely to be.

The solution is simple: leave the room.

If you do leave the room, you will probably find that the level of involvement (and noise) increases almost immediately and when you return that the atmosphere has been busier, more wholehearted and more active than when you left.

But the value of leaving the room is not restricted to structured exercises. Conventional unstructured discussions can often benefit from the teacher leaving the room for part or even all of the time. In a tutorial where you felt that the students would benefit from your leaving the room you might say, for example, 'I feel this session isn't going very well and I feel uncomfortable about it. I think I'm saying too much and dominating too much and I don't think this is very helpful to you. What I'm going to do now is leave and let you continue on your own. I suggest that you take one item at a time and proceed as you see fit. Maria and James, could you please act as observers and notice how the session goes, reporting back very briefly to the group when we meet again next week. Thanks. I'll see you then. Goodbye'. Having once taken responsibility for handling their own group, students may afterwards behave more productively and take more initiative in teacher-led groups.

33   Carry on without me

This is an extension of **Leave the room** (see previous item).

There are times when teachers are unable to meet their students because they need to attend a conference or meeting, for example, or because they are ill. Often they cancel their seminars and tutorials or, if they don't actually cancel them, they send instructions to the students to 'get on with something', which the students interpret as cancellation.

In fact your absence gives the students an excellent opportunity to take more responsibility for their own learning and to have the kind of discussion which your presence might inhibit.

If they are not used to carrying on without you, they will need to be introduced to the idea. In the case of a seminar, there should be no problem: you can say, 'We've got a programme planned for the next six weeks with one student taking responsibility for each week. I'd like to emphasise the fact that I don't have to be here for the seminar to take place. I may miss one seminar for a meeting and I'd like to impress upon you the fact that I expect you to carry on without me. How do you feel about that?'

In the case of a tutorial, you could say, 'Over the winter months people get colds and 'flu and it's obviously possible that I might be off sick one day. It would be a terrible waste if you just went away when you found I wasn't there. You could run your own tutorial based on the programme we've arranged for the term or you could discuss the lecture or you could do whatever seemed to be a good idea. Let me ask you now, if you'd got an e-mail this morning saying I wasn't coming in today, what could you have usefully done in the tutorial?'

The discussion can then lead on to the students making a commitment to carry on without you if you are absent. This commitment could form part of a group agreement (see item 3). You could also establish that group members check their e-mail accounts every day. If you do have to be absent, you could then e-mail the students and remind them of their agreement to carry on the work without you.

34 Self-help groups

One of the limitations imposed on tutorials by both teachers and students is the assumption that they occur only when they are scheduled on the timetable and when the teacher is present. Since, implicitly and explicitly, we value collaborative work so highly, it seems to make sense to encourage students to move beyond this limitation by meeting in self-help groups without staff guidance and outside scheduled tutorial time.

A self-help group can consist of all the members of your tutorial group or of a sub-group, or sub-groups, within it.

If you introduce your students to the idea of self-help groups, you will find that some of them respond positively and may even be already operating an informal system of self help. Others, who have been influenced by the emphasis on secrecy and competition in traditional education, will be less enthusiastic and will need to be reassured about cheating and plagiarism.

How they spend their time in the self-help sessions is, of course, up to the students, though you can be helpful in various ways when they first set up their groups. You can recommend procedures for the group such as:

a   when the group meets, members agree a rough agenda, a timetable, and a time to finish;

b   when a meeting finishes, members do not leave without fixing a time and place for the next meeting;

c   the group chooses a 'secretary' who takes responsibility for the above.

You can suggest suitable activities for the group, such as: reading one another's essays, exchanging views about set books, comparing lecture notes, and generally trying out their ideas, and giving one another support and encouragement. You can also help with practical arrangements, such as room booking, and give support generally by showing an interest in the progress of the group.

The likely benefits to students from belonging to a self-help group are an increase in confidence and autonomy and the building of collaborative relationships.

35 A new teacher

If you want your students collectively to take responsibility for a tutorial, but you know that your presence is likely to lead the students to look to you for answers or leadership, you could absent yourself (see items 32 and 33).

However, groups of students sometimes do not work very well without a teacher as leader. This can be the case when the subject matter of the tutorial is difficult or complicated, the students lack interest or enthusiasm for a topic, the groups are large, or when there are certain members of the group who like to take over or sabotage non-led work.

In such situations, you could ask one of your colleagues to take your tutorial (of course you'll need to return the favour). Depending on the necessities of the session, it can be productive to ask a colleague with no or very little knowledge of the area your group is learning about. That way, the students can organise discussions and inform the teacher about the area while the teacher can take control of the group if the students go off track.

36 Group grades

Many teachers would like to encourage co-operation and team-work by getting their students to do group projects but feel hampered by the problem of assessment: they are afraid that, if they award separate grades to individual members of the group, not only will they have difficulty judging individual contributions but also by differentiating between students they will threaten the trust and co-operation in the group.

The alternative, of giving the same grade to every member of the group, often strikes students as being unfair: the hard workers feel that the lazy members are bringing down the standard of the group and taking advantage of others.

A working compromise is to award a group grade which the students divide up among themselves. For example, a group of 6 students may produce a group project report which gains a mark of 62 per cent. The group is then given 62 × 6 marks = 372 marks to divide up between its members as it sees fit.

The advantages of this method are that the marks are being allocated by those who are in the best position to judge individual contributions and that students are taking responsibility for decisions affecting their team. The group may of course decide to divide up the marks equally whatever happens; this is their decision and they are likely to learn from it.

Chapter 6

Evaluating the work of the group

37 Group self-monitoring   87

38 Observers   89

39 Checking it out   91

40 Record your tutorial   93

41 Consulting the group   95

37 Group self-monitoring

Students usually know when things are going badly in a group. And they are normally in a better position than the teacher to identify the causes. What they generally lack is some kind of procedure for dealing with the situation.

Teachers in various institutions have developed questionnaires to help students monitor the working of their groups. There is a wide range of these but the simplest and most flexible consists of two sheets of paper which are blank except for the headings '**What's going wrong in this group?**' and '**What's going right in this group?**' Students write their own answers to the two questions and then the group uses this material as the basis for discussion.

A more structured way of using these question sheets is the pyramid (see item **17**). The stages of the pyramid could be:

a   individuals write answers to the questions;

b   pairs compare answers and identify problem areas;

c   groups of four discuss possible solutions;

d   the representative from each group of four presents proposals to the total group;

e   the total group selects proposals.

(An example may be useful here. Students may feel, for instance, that there are cliques within the group and that this is causing feelings of exclusion and resentment. They may decide that the answer is for group members to sit in a different place for each tutorial.)

If you feel there are students who are unlikely to express their ideas and feelings, you could ask all students to write their suggestions down, fold their piece of paper in half and hand it to you. You could then select a piece of paper at random and the group could discuss what it says. An alternative is for you to ask all students to e-mail you their feedback at the end of one tutorial, as this gives the students more time to think about their comments and means that you can look through them in your own time before deciding what you want to discuss with the group at the next tutorial.

Group self-monitoring need not take place during tutorial time, or with the teacher present. You could encourage students to run the exercise themselves and take responsibility for their own group. If, however, their recommendations for improvement involve you, you need to be receptive to their ideas and serious in giving consideration to their suggestions.

The value of expending time and effort on this exercise will depend partly on how long the group is to stay together, though individuals can carry forward into new groups the benefits of increased awareness of group dynamics.

38 Observers

An observer's view of a situation is usually quite different from those of participants in that situation. The observer's view tends to be broader, more selective and more objective. It is worthwhile getting one or two members of your tutorial group to act as observers of their fellow students on occasions when this kind of overview would be useful.

The kind of tutorial which lends itself to this treatment is one which is operating at two clearly distinct levels: at the level of the particular, group members may be discussing the details of a case or an example or an artefact; at a more general level, their discussion is based on principles, theories, criteria, issues, etc., of which they may not be aware. Observers, by remaining apart, are in a good position to extract these broader aspects from the discussion and feed them back to the group.

The observers will probably find it easier to carry out their role if they position themselves physically apart from the rest of the group and make notes, perhaps on a flipchart sheet, as the discussion proceeds. It is important that you agree a clear title for their notes so that they know exactly what they are to look out for. Such a title might be

'General principles which underpin the discussion' or

'Criteria on which the group bases its decisions' or

'Issues arising from the case study'.

As an alternative, you can tape-record your tutorial and then play the recording to the group, all of whom will act as observers. This has the advantage that it gives everyone practice in developing observer skills. (See also item **40**.)

39 Checking it out

Teachers are often heard to make comments about groups of their students like 'They find it very difficult' or 'I don't know how to get their interest' or 'It's not going as well as last year'. Usually these comments are well founded in the sense that when the teacher feels that something is wrong, something generally is; the signs of discontent are not hard to read. But the mistake that teachers often make is to expect to be able to judge exactly what is wrong without actually checking it out with the students themselves and asking them. These teachers run the risk of mistaking students' exhaustion for boredom, puzzlement for hostility, thoughtfulness for laziness, and so on.

There are various ways in which you can check things out with your students. For example, if you want to get some quick feedback about your tutorials you can say, 'I'm feeling a bit unclear about what you think about the tutorials so far this term. So I'd like to suggest that we go round and everyone says one positive and one negative thing – one thing you've liked and one thing you haven't. I'll start, to show you what I mean' (see item 22). Or, in a less structured form, 'I'm worried about the work we've done so far this term in this group. I feel I'm not getting through to you. How do you feel about it?' If your students are likely to be afraid to take individual responsibility for this kind of feedback, they could perhaps have five minutes' discussion in groups of two or three and appoint a spokesperson to speak on behalf of each group, or each student could anonymously write their thoughts down and give their paper to you to select comments at random.

If in a tutorial you ask a question and nobody answers, you could gloss over the fact by answering it yourself or by asking a further question or, alternatively, you can check out why the students didn't answer. You can say, 'Nobody's answering the question.

Is that because it isn't a very good question?' and if still nobody answers, 'Maya, would you like to say something about this?'

Checking it out with individuals can also be very helpful – and revealing. You might say, for instance, 'You look fed up today, Simon. Are you?' or 'You look puzzled, Sam. Can I help?' or 'You look as if you've had a good idea, Hayley. Can we hear it?'

40   Record your tutorial

If you want to review or analyse some aspect of your tutorial – to calculate how much time you spend speaking compared with the students, for example, or to see how long those silences really are – or if you just want to see what the tutorial looks like from outside, you can video it.

The best results are obtained from using two cameras, although a single camera can be fine for a small group (see **19 Furniture**). Alternatively, you could use a voice recorder but of course if you have sound only, you miss everything that is to be learned from seeing the body language of the group. You can, however, get a long way with very simple equipment. Your IT unit will probably be keen to assist.

Before you start you should explain to the group your reasons for making the recording and you should show it to them afterwards. Indeed, you will get far more value from it if you watch it with them and ask for their comments. They will be able to give you useful feedback on their perceptions of the tutorial.

The type of feedback you want will depend on your reasons for making the recording in the first place but these are some structured exercises with general applicability:

a   The group watches the recording and then each student suggests one thing you could do to improve the tutorial and one thing she could do. These suggestions can be spoken or written.

b   Play the recording, stop it at an important point (e.g. at a point where you asked a question and were met by silence) and then ask all the students to say what they were thinking at that moment and tell them what you were thinking.

c   The group watches the recording. Any participant can stop it and recall what was significant for her at that point. The difference between this and b, above, is that here the stop button is controlled by the students, who are in the best position to judge where in the tutorial things went right or wrong.

d   Play the recording and get pairs of students to analyse different aspects of the tutorial such as body language, how many times each group member spoke, evidence of objectives, types of question asked (see item **28**), etc.

These exercises need not be too time-consuming. You don't have to watch the recording of the whole tutorial. The first few minutes are in fact often the most important and revealing. It will probably always be useful to upload the video on the intranet so that students can watch it back in their own time.

41 Consulting the group

Teachers often have the experience of feeling unsure what to do, even in a carefully planned tutorial, either because time is running out or because there is a choice of directions which the group could take or because something unexpected happens. Usually, however, they try to conceal this uncertainty from the students: they make a quick unilateral decision about how to proceed and carry on as if nothing has happened. If, instead, they consulted the group, they would have the benefit of the views of those people who are in the best position to advise.

If you want to consult your group at a time like this, you could say, 'We seem to have taken longer than I anticipated so far. I had planned to do x and y as well. There's probably only time for one of them. Which shall we do?'

After students have got used to taking some responsibility in this way, they are likely to start suggesting courses of action, and alternatives to those you suggest. For example, in response to the above question, they might say, 'Neither, thanks. We'd like to spend the rest of the time discussing what we've done so far'.

Once you have established this kind of student involvement, you can design your sessions in a much more open-ended and flexible way, and spend less time worrying about them beforehand.

Chapter 7

Written material

42 Display   99

43 Group charts   101

44 Students' notes   103

45 Handouts   105

46 Writing   107

47 Open-book tutorials   109

48 Essay preparation   111

49 Coursework feedback   113

42 Display

Blackboards, whiteboards and presentation slides are frequently used in lectures to display material and can be very helpful to students: even a few words or a simple diagram can clarify anything from simple spellings to complex concepts and relationships.

Displaying verbal or visual material can be equally helpful in tutorials. You can display your objectives (see item 5), the agenda, an ongoing summary of the discussion or a set of headings to serve as the basis for the students' own notes. This not only clarifies things generally but also gives an opportunity for those who get left behind to catch up. At the simplest level, if students can see how unfamiliar words and names are spelt, they will feel more confident about using them and looking them up in indexes, library catalogues and online.

One reason why teachers tend not to display material in tutorials seems to be that they feel that the use of a board is too formal for what is a relatively informal teaching situation. If you feel too authoritarian writing on the board, consider bringing your students into the activity (see also item 19). You could say, 'That's a good idea, Louise. Would you like to add it to the list on the board?' or 'That'll be a new word to people in the group, Dave. Can you write it up on the board for us, please?'

See also **43 Group charts**.

43 Group charts

It's always interesting to experiment with presenting material visually. Many students will find it easier to understand a concept or model or set of relationships if you present it in the form of a diagram. The notion of the group chart is a particular application of this and is based on the technique of patterned note taking developed by Tony Buzan.[1]

Patterned or organic notes begin with a central idea in the middle of the page and work outwards along lines of association. The material is organised on the page according to links, contrasts, groupings and parallels. These can be emphasised by means of arrows and other symbols, by varying the thickness of the lines and by the use of different coloured pens. An example of a set of patterned notes is given overleaf.

This method, which some of your students probably already use for their personal notes, can be adapted for use by the group as a whole. You can begin by writing the theme of the tutorial in the middle of the board or of a sheet of flipchart paper and then invite individuals to add the lines of association as these arise in discussion. For example, in the illustration overleaf, the chart began with the central theme of 'non-verbal communication' and students who introduced the areas of 'books', 'benefits', 'dangers', etc. added them to the chart. For people who have worked on such a chart and explored the relationships within it, this method of presenting material is much more meaningful than a simple list of items would be. It also serves as a model for students when they are assembling ideas for essays.

Writing on flipchart sheets rather than on the board means that when a theme continues over more than one week, the students can carry on where they left off and also that you can store all the charts and display them for revision purposes at the end of the course.

Reference

1 Buzan , T., *Use Your Head*, BBC Active, 2006.

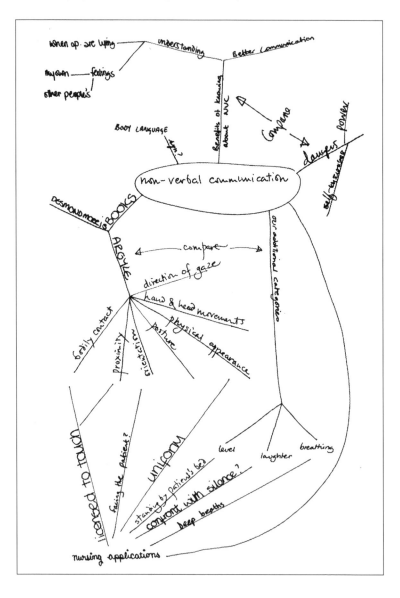

44 Students' notes

It is even more difficult for students to take notes in seminars and tutorials than in lectures. The main problems are that it is virtually impossible to participate in a discussion at the same time as keeping a written record of it and also that it is very difficult in a free-ranging and loosely constructed discussion to keep track of the main arguments.

You can help your students with their notes in a number of ways:

a   Acknowledge that there's a problem and encourage them to discuss it and suggest solutions for themselves.

b   Where a seminar or tutorial has a predetermined structure, indicate this on a chart or handout.

c   Be generous with handouts. Give students copies of references, quotations, questions, diagrams or calculations (see item 45).

d   Encourage students to interrupt the discussion in order to ask for clarification or time to note things down.

either:

e   Summarise what is said or get one of the students to summarise, either at the end or at selected points during the tutorial.

or:

f   At the end of the tutorial get everyone to write down 'The three most important things in today's tutorial' and write three yourself. These can be listed on the board and form the basis of students' notes.

or:

g   Do a round of 'What I'm taking away from this tutorial' (see item **22**). These contributions, again, can be listed on the board and students can be given five minutes to copy them down.

45 Handouts

Handouts can be very helpful in indicating structures and serving as a focal point for discussion as well as saving students the unrewarding labour of copying quotations, etc.

Handouts can contain any of the following:

a   lists or charts of the material or activities to be covered in the course as a whole or in particular tutorials;

b   a list of references which students are to follow up;

c   a passage or set of quotations to be discussed;

d   a set of opposing arguments to be debated (see item **18**);

e   a set of questions with spaces in which students write answers;

f   a set of headings with numbers for students to list points:

Advantages   *Disadvantages*

1.............   1.............
2.............   2.............
3.............   3.............

g   problems or calculations;

h   a summary of the previous week's session. (Where this was a student-led seminar, the student concerned can write the summary.)

46 Writing

Apart from any notes they may take, students tend to do very little writing in tutorials. And teachers tend not to encourage them to write, possibly because writing is slower than speaking and tutorial time is precious. But if you leave writing off your agenda, not only does this restrict the scope of the tutorial, but also it contradicts the emphasis which is placed on written work when it comes to assessment.

This is not a recommendation that students write instead of speaking but that writing becomes one of the range of regular ways in which they express themselves. It seems to work particularly well at the start of the tutorial because it helps students to gather their thoughts and sort out their ideas before engaging in open discussion. If you join in yourself, both you and your students will get more out of it.

Some ways of using writing in tutorials:

a   *Key words*
Everyone writes down an agreed number of key words (say 6, or 10) on the tutorial topic. The tutorial agenda can then be derived from the total list. You can start, for example, by writing all the key words on the board and then rank them in order of importance or group them according to common characteristics. Advantages of this method are that it generates a lot of material from the group in a short time, it focuses people's attention on the essentials, and it provides a useful basis for later revision.

b   *Write before you speak*
You ask students the kind of question you would ordinarily ask in a tutorial but everyone writes down their response

rather than saying it. The advantage of this method is that all students have time to work out their answers and have something concrete to contribute to the discussion.

c   *Pass it round*
Everyone writes something on a topic or in answer to a question. After an agreed time they pass their papers round and make notes on each other's contributions. These notes then form the basis for the discussion. This method is suitable for a situation where you want to illustrate the variety of viewpoints or angles represented in the tutorial group.

The timing of these exercises is important. The amount of time that students need will obviously vary according to the topic, the size of the group, the individuals in the group, etc. but as a general guide, the writing part of the exercises described above will probably take (a) 5 minutes (b) 10 minutes and (c) 10 + 30 = 40 minutes. You will need to organise the session in such a way that there is enough time both for writing and for discussion.

Some students may be hesitant about committing their ideas to paper. You can help them to reduce such hesitation by:

i   making it clear that all writing in the early stages will be 'private' (e.g. between pairs of students);

ii   basing writing tasks on personal views or experience rather than specialist knowledge which can be judged to be right or wrong;

iii using writing frequently as a means of direct communication rather than only when students are assessed.

47   Open-book tutorials

One reason why teachers are often met by silences when they ask questions in tutorials is that students have quite simply forgotten what they are supposed to have learned from lectures and books.

If your students seem to forget things easily and you don't want the success of your tutorials to depend on their memories, you could try open book tutorials. The name comes from open book examinations, which are sometimes held in such subjects as literature. Candidates are allowed to use their textbooks in the examination room, on the grounds that they are being tested on their critical and analytic skills rather than on their ability to memorise material.

A tutorial in which you encourage students to refer to books and notes will have a different focus in that students' initial response to your questions will be to start turning over pages and reading. But because students will not be spending their time anxiously trying to remember the written material, the atmosphere will be more relaxed and the level of thinking and discussion will be higher.

48 Essay preparation

If writing essays is to be a learning experience, students should not have to wait until the essay is returned to discover that they have made fundamental errors at the planning stage. Many teachers are aware of this and one way in which they try to ensure that students are working within a useful framework is by telling them what the framework should be. There are two disadvantages in this method: one is that the teacher is doing the work for the students and the other is that the method doesn't allow for the great variation in students' approaches to the task.

If you want to use some tutorial time for essay preparation, a way of involving all members of the group and benefiting from the variety of approaches is to get students to make a plan for the essay individually and then share their ideas. This sharing can be done by each group member in turn holding up his/her plan and explaining it. (If the group is too large this can be done in subgroups.) Or, as an alternative, group members can pair off, read each other's plan and then do a round (see item **22**) of 'What I liked about my neighbour's plan' or 'How I would summarise my neighbour's plan'.

If your students are worried about other people stealing their best ideas, you can get them to do this exercise with non-assessed essay questions or past examination questions until they get used to sharing.

49   Coursework feedback

Sometimes, every student writes an essay or piece of coursework on something different and pieces of work can be extremely lengthy. During such cases, giving feedback on the coursework in the tutorial is not ideal because every person's feedback will be different. However, it may be useful to spend a small amount of time explaining common errors, such as problems in referencing or layout.

On the other hand, if the work has a relatively short word limit (for example, up to 2000 words) and if the group were set just one or two coursework titles, or the content of the work will be well known to all the other students, tutorials can be used to great effect when it comes to providing feedback. Upon handing back the work, there are a number of follow up options:

a   Spend a small amount of time going through common errors and successes. Then split the group up and give one-to-one feedback on specific problem areas (this may require spending time outside the allocated tutorial period if groups are large). This way, you will not waste time in the one-to-one feedback repeating all the common issues.

b   Get students to read the work of other people. (This is probably best when the essays are identified only by a number, or when the group is very trusting of one another.) After everyone has read two or three pieces of work, a round (see item 22) can be used asking everyone to identify something good they noticed in the work or something they themselves hadn't thought of or the areas in which they think there are common weaknesses.

c   Hand out copies of a sample piece of coursework that you have prepared. Allow students to compare their work to that of the sample before discussing the strengths of the sample and what the students missed out.

d   Encourage students to form self-help groups (see item 34) outside the tutorial so that they can read and comment on one another's work.

Chapter 8

Expressing feelings

50 What's on top   117

51 Self disclosure   119

52 Praise and encouragement   121

53 Concluding   123

50 What's on top

The substantive topic of a tutorial is not the only thing on the minds of group members, nor necessarily the most important. It can be very useful to have a round (see item 22) at the start of a tutorial to allow group members to share those thoughts and feelings which are on their minds: something hanging over from the previous week, the experience of reading an exciting book, telling the others about a TV documentary relevant to the course, or simply saying, 'I've got a cold, so I may not be too quick this afternoon'. These brief offerings may or may not be very important or interesting to other members of the group but will preoccupy the person involved for the whole of the tutorial unless they are expressed early on.

With in-service groups of teachers, managers, nurses, etc. who are meeting in a learning group in the context of continuing work and professional practice, the opportunity to express what's 'on top' may be an excellent way of linking the course with their work. If group members know they will have the opportunity to share experiences and feelings in this way, they are more likely to notice things at work and store them up for the start of the next group meeting. Sometimes, in fact, 'What's on top?' becomes the most important part of the group's activities.

If you are worried that too much of your tutorial time will be taken up in this way, you can of course set a time limit of one or two minutes on each member's contribution.

51 Self disclosure

Students get a lot of help and encouragement from teachers' self disclosure. Probably the two most helpful things that teachers can do as self disclosure are to express their feelings and admit to their limitations.

If as a teacher you have a strong feeling about something and you don't express it verbally it will be a distraction both to you and to your students. If you do express it, this will help to dispel the feeling and also serve as an example which your students can follow when expressing their feelings themselves. Indeed, it hardly seems fair to ask students to do things which you are not prepared to do yourself.

Admitting to their limitations is something which many teachers strenuously avoid. They think that if they show what they imagine to be weakness, their students will lose faith in them. In fact, students have no trouble recognising cover-ups and show respect for teachers who are honest and don't pretend to be perfect. Ways in which you can admit to your limitations are to say, 'I'm sorry. I don't understand that' or 'I don't know the answer to that question' or 'I haven't read that book. Who wrote it?' or 'Yes, I get worried about that sort of thing too'. And a simple practical favour you can do your students is to show them a rough draft of something you've written complete with crossings out and alterations; they will find it very comforting.

52 Praise and encouragement

Teachers can often be heard talking about their students and saying how much they've learned from individuals, how nice a particular group is, how well their students work, etc. but these views are rarely expressed to the students themselves. This is a pity because groups work together more harmoniously and produce better results when the members feel good about themselves.

It is a good idea to look for opportunities to give praise and encouragement to your groups, particularly if you characteristically spend time in tutorials criticising and correcting students' contributions. If you are pleased with how they are getting on, say so. You could say, 'We're making a lot of progress on this course' or 'I think you've worked really well today' or 'What we've been doing this morning has been quite tricky so you've done well to keep at it and not give up'. If you feel that you can't honestly praise the whole session, then you could say, 'We've had our problems this afternoon but I really liked the way you tackled x'. There is always something positive you can find to say once you start looking.

If you want to involve the students themselves in this positive thinking about the group, you can suggest that they make a list of 'what we've achieved this term' or 'what we like about being in this group' or 'six good ideas we've had in this group', etc.

53 Concluding

During the academic year teachers and students may spend upwards of 100 hours in each other's company in what is both an academic and a social experience.

A formal conclusion to this joint experience can serve important academic functions: you and your students can draw together themes covered in earlier weeks, state conclusions and reflect knowledgeably upon issues which the course has raised. If there is a post-course examination this concluding session can be particularly valuable for helping students with their revision if some question and answer time is included.

A formal conclusion can also serve important social functions to do with bringing the formal working relationship to an end. This is an opportunity for the group to break up in a positive atmosphere with any loose ends tied up and to express good fellowship and exchange good wishes for the future.

You could introduce this session as follows and lead on to a round (see item 22):

'Since this is the last session it would be nice to finish in a positive way so let's all say one thing we've liked about being in this group this year. I'll say one too. Who'd like to start?'

Printed in the United States
by Baker & Taylor Publisher Services